MW01156899

1UU1

SEX SECRETS
EVERY MAN
SHOULD KNOW

Other Avon Books
Researched by
Chris Allen

1001 SEX SECRETS EVERY WOMAN SHOULD KNOW

1001

SEX SECRETS
EVERY MAN
SHOULD KNOW

Researched by
CHRIS ALLEN

AVON BOOKS ◆ NEW YORK

AVON BOOKS
A division of
The Hearst Corporation
1350 Avenue of the Americas
New York, New York 10019

Copyright © 1992 by Creative Fire
Published by arrangement with Creative Fire
Library of Congress Catalog Card Number: 94-23333
ISBN: 0-380-72483-9

Library of Congress Cataloging in Publication Data:
Allen, Chris. 1963-
  1001 sex secrets every man should know / researched by Chris Allen.
    p.   cm.
1. Sex—Miscellanea. 2. Women—Sexual behavior—Miscellanea. I. Title.
II. Title: One thousand one sex secrets every man should know. III. Title: One thousand and one sex secrets every man should know.
HQ23.A425   1992   94-23333
306.7—dc20   CIP

First Avon Books Trade Printing: February 1995

AVON TRADEMARK REG. U.S. PAT. OFF. AND IN OTHER COUNTRIES, MARCA REGISTRADA, HECHO EN U.S.A.

Printed in the U.S.A.

OPM 10 9 8 7 6 5 4 3 2 1

Preface

The following material was obtained over a period of twenty-four months. The participants were selected at random. Responses were gathered through face-to-face conversations, telephone interviews and written correspondence. While many women were comfortable volunteering their insights without prompting, others chose to express themselves through the completion of sentences such as: "I love it when...," "The perfect man knows that...," "The one thing I wish my husband/boyfriend knew about sex is...," and so on. This project was never intended to be a psychological, sociological or clinical study, nor was it intended to serve as an accurate representation of the female population. The only thing it was ever meant to be was REAL.

1001
SEX SECRETS
EVERY MAN
SHOULD KNOW

1.

I love to step out of the shower and he's waiting there to dry me off.

--Vicky, 26

2.

Men need to lighten up and have fun in bed.

--Sharon, 31

3.

When we're having dinner alone together, I really get into little finger foods we can feed each other.

--Amanda, 22

4._____

I can't breathe when a man lays on
top of me.

--Hanna, 35

5._____

I love orgasms, but I don't have to
have one to have a good time in bed.

--Nona, 38

6._____

Men are so selfish. I want one that
cares about my needs.

--Polly, 32

_____

7.

I love a man who will ease me into lovemaking.

--Laura, 37

8.

When you come to bed, don't forget your sense of humor.

--Patricia, 29

9.

I love it when my husband treats me like it's our first time again. He's so loving and gentle.

--Beth, 41

10._____

I need to be touched and held more than I need an orgasm.

--Amie, 34

11._____

I like it when I can tell a man how I feel and know that he won't laugh at me.

--Lisa, 37

12._____

I'm constantly wondering how I look. It puts me at ease when he tells me I'm beautiful.

--Carolyn, 40

_____

_____13.

Sometimes I just like to snuggle for a while. That's still lovemaking to me.

--Yvonne, 30

_____14.

I don't want to do it when I don't feel fresh and pretty.

--Maxine, 28

_____15.

Doing it in a public place is such a rush.

--Tiffany, 24

16.

I like having my hair brushed after we've just made love.

--Ann Marie, 31

17.

Waking up to a man kissing my body, or doing something else, is like waking up in heaven.

--Deedee, 41

18.

My husband picks out little areas of my body and compliments me on them.

--Kara, 32

_____**19.**

Lovemaking is extra-special in the morning. I feel like I've got a secret all day.

--Kelly, 32

_____**20.**

I'd rather do it in a Jacuzzi than in a bed.

--Debra, 21

_____**21.**

I like a long, leisurely bubble bath before.

--Jill, 39

_____

22.

I like for my lovers to share their fantasies with me.

--Tracie, 43

23.

Sometimes it's about his pleasure and sometimes it's about mine.

--Freda, 36

24.

One time my boyfriend blindfolded me and drove out to one of those kinky motels. It was great.

--Nina, 27

25.

My boyfriend and I like to get out
the Poloriod and take some very
private pictures of each other.

--Mary, 37

26.

We have special names for each
other when we make love.

--Nancy, 25

27.

When a man uses his tongue gently, I
know he's going to be a good lover.

--Helen, 32

28._____

I hate doing it after a heavy meal. I can't feel sexy when my stomach's full.

--Cheryl, 38

29._____

Most guys are so fidgety in bed. They need to relax so I can, too.

--Jeanie, 32

30._____

I never get tired of hearing how pretty you think I am.

--Janine, 38

31.

I don't get any pleasure from oral sex--but I'll do it for him.

--Sarah, 29

32.

Some guys crank their stereos up like we're going to do it in a rock video. That's annoying.

--Rene, 21

33.

Focus your attention on me--not the TV.

--Karen, 27

34.

Please, please, please don't use cheap cologne.

--Gerry, 28

35.

Let me know what I'm doing right, not just what's wrong.

--Kim, 29

36.

Sometimes I like to leave my panties on and have him pull them to one side.

--Shiela, 34

37.

On a boat is great. It's like the waves know you're making love and want to help you.

--Brenda, 25

38.

My sweetheart leaves me notes when he's in the mood. They're as sweet and sexy as he is.

--Darlene, 33

39.

We like to make an appointment to have sex. And there's no cancelling.

--Jill, 36

40._____

Nothing out of *9 1/2 Weeks*.

--Beth, 31

41._____

I love it when my husband wants to have sex in the morning. What a great way to start the day.

--Jenny, 36

42._____

I need more affection after sex than before.

--Barbara, 35

_____

43.

I don't think guys should wear that much jewelry anyway, but I don't want any on him in bed.

--Theresa, 29

44.

Just because a man takes me to dinner doesn't mean he's paid for the right to sleep with me.

--Kim, 23

45.

I like to slow-dance nude with my boyfriend for starters.

--Rhonda, 31

46._____

My favorite place to make love is
in front of the fireplace.

--Diedre, 31

47._____

I'm into sex anywhere but in bed.

--Lizzie, 23

48._____

I'm not using my period as an
excuse to avoid sex.

--Elizabeth, 37

49.

Sometimes men put on these big macho acts. I wish they knew I'm not impressed.

--Linda, 38

50.

Read me something sexy to get me going.

--Annie, 24

51.

The man I'm with has to have a great butt. I know that's sexist, but I don't care.

--Heather, 22

52._____

No food in bed.

--Abbie, 37

53._____

When I'm feeling particularly
naughty, a little bare-bottom
spanking is in order.

--Allison, 26

54._____

Feathers can be lots of fun.

--Paige, 30

_____

55.

After eleven, I need time for myself. If we haven't done it by then, it's not going to happen.

--Leanne, 30

56.

When my boyfriend starts making love to me the same way all the time is when I start looking.

--Tracy, 28

57.

After we make love, my husband surprises me with a little gift.

--Sandra, 41

58.

When we're on the dancefloor together, it should be like foreplay.

--Cindee, 24

59.

Talk dirty to me.

--Mary, 27

60.

Having my hair stroked really gets me in the mood.

--Clarice, 32

61.

I hate it when a man pulls out immediately after orgasm.

--Maria, 32

62.

I like it when my boyfriend talks to me in a low, deep voice. It's like I'm with a stranger.

--Katie, 27

63.

A lot of men are pushovers because they're so intent on getting laid. That's boring.

--Caroline, 25

64._____

I like to leave the blinds wide
open.

--Bunny, 38

65._____

Hot breath in my ear gives me
goosebumps.

--Kris, 33

66._____

Oral sex only after a few drinks.

--Gena, 28

_____

67.

I like a man who isn't afraid to show me his vulnerable side.

--Molly, 29

68.

So many men expect sex right away. Can't we just have a nice night out for once?

--Susan, 31

69.

It's rare to find a man who will perform oral sex as gently and delicately as I like it.

--Penny, 37

70.

Having my toes massaged puts me into orbit.

--Patty, 28

71.

Performing in front of each other can sometimes be more fun than with each other.

--Taylor, 24

72.

It's amazing where men expect you to put your mouth when they haven't even showered.

--Suzanne, 34

73.

There's a difference between being touched and being pawed.

--Monica, 32

74.

I want the man to be in control during sex. If I'm on top, I'm too self-conscious.

--Valerie, 28

75.

I can't enjoy sex when I know the kids are due in. I wish my husband understood.

--Kate, 33

76.

A man who works hard deserves to be loved hard.

--Jessica, 26

77.

I feel like it's the man's job to seduce me. I'm not going to make the first move.

--Christine, 32

78.

He likes to leave the lights on. I don't mind as long as he tells me I look great.

--Karen, 36

79.

Self-confidence in a man is sexy.
Cockiness is a real turn-off.

--Becky, 29

80.

Music goes a long way in setting the
proper mood for lovemaking.

--Donna, 24

81.

Slow and easy is all I have to say.

--Robin, 30

82._____

When a man uses his tongue and hands to please me, he's got to know the difference between making love and a cavity search.

--Terri, 34

83._____

I can't tolerate a stinky man in bed.

--Ruth, 31

84._____

Sex and love are the same in that you're only going to get out of it what you're willing to put in.

--Cecilia, 37

_____**85.**

Flowers never fail to get my
attention.

--Jackie, 42

_____**86.**

As long as you treat each other with
as much love as you did in the
beginning, the sex can't help but be
great.

--Karla, 40

_____**87.**

Be my friend first, then my lover.

--Sue, 31

_____

88.

You can do amazing things with peanut butter (not crunchy, though).

--Maryanne, 30

89.

The secret to great sex is honesty. No illusions, just the truth.

--Mindy, 27

90.

Want sex? I want a ring.

--Roz, 26

91.

Some mornings my husband brings me champagne in bed and then wakes me up with kisses all over.

--Quinn, 31

92.

Orgasm is difficult for me. If I don't climax, my husband doesn't take it personally.

--Shelly, 28

93.

I love taking a shower together. Soaping each other up gets me hot.

--Nicki, 26

94.

Giving myself to a man sexually is the greatest gift I can give. He must appreciate it.

--Lena, 34

95.

It's not always about who comes and how frequently.

--Faith, 29

96.

There are times when I'm totally giving. Other times I just want to get.

--Joanne, 31

97.

I want to be touched before, during, after and outside of sex.

--Penny, 35

98.

My boyfriend licks around my nipples and then blows on them. They get hard immediately.

--Christine, 22

99.

A man who is proud to be with me helps me like myself. Then I can like him.

--Morgan, 28

100._____

I really don't enjoy oral sex, but
I'll do it if it means a lot to him.

--Brenda, 28

101._____

He always wants to do it right after
we've eaten. I need time to digest.

--Sue, 34

102._____

I need some coaxing, attention and
time to get ready.

--Melonie, 36

_____

103.

Sixty-nine is my favorite thing.
But only if I'm on top or we're
both on our sides.

--Marcy, 26

104.

Hold me all night long.

--Julie, 23

105.

I enjoy watching X-rated videos
with my husband, but I don't like
the lesbian scenes. It should just be
men with women.

--Anna, 39

106.

I love my husband to tell me how wonderful it feels inside me.

--Katie, 32

107.

Clean socks and underwear are a must.

--Rozena, 35

108.

Slow going in, then fast coming out. I've taught every man I've ever had to do it like that.

--Rita, 39

109.

A man who is sensitive to my feelings is the only kind of man I can give myself to.

--Joan, 35

110.

Hand-holding is very underrated.

--Kim, 24

111.

Sex doesn't always have to be an act of love, but it's best when it is.

--Carrie, 31

112._____

Hairy backs gross me out.

--Marlee, 24

113._____

Dripping candle wax hurts so good.

--Felicia, 32

114._____

I don't want to be a lady in the bedroom; I want to be bad.

--Adrian, 36

_____

115.

I hate it when sex becomes part of a routine, like "Wednesday night is sex night." Where's the fun in that?

--Sabrina, 31

116.

If a guy's just looking for a piece of ass, he can look somewhere else.

--Darlene, 22

117.

We like to tease each other until we're practically dying for it.

--Michelle, 27

118._____

Falling asleep in my husband's arms is my favorite.

--Verlinda, 34

119._____

A man who enjoys laughing is a very sexy man to me.

--Katherine, 43

120._____

Sometimes my head will be banging against the headboard and my boyfriend won't even stop. That pisses me off.

--Katrina, 26

121.

Things can get quite interesting with a bowl of lemon meringue in the bed.

--Phyllis, 32

122.

I've always fantisized about two men at once. Maybe someday.

--Lilly, 34

123.

I love surprises, especially in bed.

--Linda, 21

124.

The man I married makes love to me every day with his words and his kindness.

--Faye, 37

125.

If we're going to do it on the carpet, we put down a blanket so we don't get rug burns.

--Trinnie, 31

126.

Don't even think about bondage or S&M.

--Morgan, 34

_____127.

The beach is the most romantic place to make love, as long as there isn't any sand on the man's penis.

--Olivia, 30

_____128.

Slower is always better.

--Grace, 43

_____129.

Use your hands all over my body. I love to have my legs stroked.

--Maureen, 37

130._____

During oral sex, my husband puts an ice cube in his mouth to keep his tongue cold.

--Regina, 33

131._____

We never go into the bedroom angry or upset. If we have a problem, we work it out before.

--Phyllis, 28

132._____

I love having my fingers sucked.

--Claudia, 44

_____

_____**133.**

My husband has some old shirts in the closet. Some nights he'll put one on so I can bite the buttons off.

--Clair, 34

_____**134.**

Any lover of mine has to be willing to fill me in on his sexual history.

--Kyra, 23

_____**135.**

Sex should be playful, not like it's the end of the world.

--Marla, 28

_____

136.

A man doesn't give me an orgasm--I have to take it.

--June, 39

137.

In the missionary position, I always slide a pillow under me. The elevation helps me feel the sensation of having him inside me.

--Sally, 43

138.

I'm always up for a new position.

--Lougina, 34

139.

I have a cardinal rule against dating any man who chews tobacco.

--Joanne, 39

140.

Men think it's so funny to point out little imperfections on my body. Nothing turns me off faster.

--Angela, 33

141.

Men with big penises are lazy in bed. Like the sheer size of it is going to make them great lovers.

--Diane, 40

142._____

A waterbed that lets you heat up the water is terrific.

--Marylin, 30

143._____

Fondle my breasts gently, as if they'd break if you were too rough.

--Kelli, 25

144._____

I used to feel guilty when I'd fantisize about other men. But it makes me feel sexy and, ultimately, that helps our marriage.

--Verdie, 42

145.

A man who gives me his undivided attention makes me feel special.

--Lorraine, 31

146.

If a man hasn't got anything in his heart, I don't care what he's got in his pants.

--Liz, 38

147.

I know I'm not perfect, but in bed I like to be treated as if I am.

--Joycelyn, 28

148._____

I'm searching for a kinder, gentler
man.

--Maxine, 38

149._____

It's a Catch-22. Men have this
anxiety about having to perform,
then because of it, they can't.

--Elvira, 35

150._____

Doing it in strange places has
become like a hobby to me.

--Marliesha, 27

151.

My husband buys me perfume that he finds attractive. I feel sexier knowing he likes how I smell.

--Annette, 34

152.

I like to share my fantasies. It's nice when you feel like you can trust someone.

--Maggie, 31

153.

Men who are not so presumptuous excite me.

--Corrine, 28

154._____

I'll be your love-slave, but you've got to be willing to reciprocate.

--Natalie, 26

155._____

The longer a man waits to get inside me, the sooner I can come.

--Bernice, 34

156._____

I need to know what you find attractive in me.

--Leola, 33

_____

157.

After lovemaking, we put lotion all over each other. By the time we're finished, we're ready to do it again.

--Nicole, 32

158.

A well-mannered gentleman is the only one I'll let near my body.

--Katrina, 29

159.

My husband shows me he loves me in non-sexual ways. That makes him even sexier to me.

--Janine, 37

160._____

I enjoy the thrill of the hunt.

--Naydene, 31

161._____

Two types of men to avoid: beeper-carriers and guys with big keyrings.

--Monica, 34

162._____

There's no rule that says only he gets to choose when we have sex. I like to pick the times, also.

--Katina, 28

_____163.

If I let a man stay over at my place,
he's got to respect my things.

--*Randi, 27*

_____164.

My boyfriend never rushes me.
That makes the sex even better.

--*Barbara, 30*

_____165.

Status symbols, like gold cards, do
not impress me. It's what a man has
inside that counts.

--*Crystal, 33*

166._____

I can't date a guy with hair longer
than mine.

--Jennifer, 24

167._____

It's the person that makes sex
special for me, not the position.

--Sandra, 32

168._____

I don't want sex, I want to make
love.

--Mysti, 25

_____

_____169.

When I'm feeling especially kinky, we'll get out the video camera and star in our own porno movies.

--Diahann, 23

_____170.

If I just order a salad, there will be no hanky-panky this evening.

--Melissa, 29

_____171.

I like it when a man is comfortable enough with himself to let me be the aggressor sometimes.

--AnnMarie, 31

172.

Be patient with me. I don't have a penis.

--Emily, 26

173.

Men I can feel safe with turn me on.

--Lauren, 29

174.

We laugh and talk after sex, and that's the real lovemaking to me.

--Deanne, 30

_____**175.**

I'd rather make it with the same guy
ten different ways than with ten
guys the same way.

--Gena, 25

_____**176.**

The sun doesn't have to go down for
you to go down on me.

--Kimberly, 26

_____**177.**

A nice, little trail of Hershey's
kisses leading to the bedroom
makes for a nice seduction.

--Beverly, 33

178._____

Mature men with a sense of humor
make the best lovers.

--Earline, 39

179._____

What's the big hurry? Take your
time.

--Lindsey, 33

180._____

I enjoy the security and comfort of
a monogamous relationship. It's
the only way I can have sex.

--Kathleen, 34

181.

I hate it when he tries to make me feel guilty for saying "no."

--Rose, 36

182.

I like it when he holds my hand and leads me into the bedroom.

--Dora, 27

183.

The rougher and more callused a man's hands, the better. I like to feel hard skin against me.

--Cybil, 34

184._____

Gold chains are boring.

--Lisa, 31

185._____

A man who appreciates my daily duties will always be appreciated by me.

--Rachel, 36

186._____

I know he loves me if he thinks I look good in the morning.

--Susie, 41

_____

_____**187.**

I like it when a man notices my
pretty little underthings.

--Charlene, 27

_____**188.**

When my boyfriend caresses my
stomach, I get real interested real
fast.

--Kate, 23

_____**189.**

I don't like for a man to tell me I
remind him of anyone else. I'm
unique.

--Diedra, 29

190.

I love laying down and having him peel my stockings off one at a time.

--Meredith, 34

191.

We just neck sometimes, like we were in high-school again.

--Kathey, 38

192.

Ask me what feels good and then do it slowly.

--Doris, 37

193.

I like a man to stay inside me after he's had an orgasm. Often, a more flacid penis stimulates me more.

--Monique, 35

194.

We give each other plenty of space in our relationship. That makes the sex even more enjoyable.

--Tammy, 31

195.

I get the greatest pleasure from pleasing my partner.

--Rhonda, 28

196.

I hate it from behind.

--Beth, 26

197.

Hold my hair while I go down on you.

--Anna, 31

198.

I like wearing my husband's clothes. They smell just like him.

--Helen, 34

_____**199.**

Making love while the sun sets is
the most romantic thing ever.

--Patsy, 30

_____**200.**

If a man truly loves me, I'll give
him whatever he wants sexually.

--Nanette, 29

_____**201.**

There's a fine line between pleasure
and pain and I like to walk it.

--Georgina, 38

202._____

Bring me breakfast in bed and I'll be your brunch.

--Carrie, 28

203._____

I take no pleasure from sex toys.

--Lonnie, 36

204._____

Flirtation is a lost art.

--Wendi, 38

_____

_____205.

Before we have sex, I like for a man
to stand totally naked in front of me
so I can see it all.

--Jill, 40

_____206.

Older men are great teachers;
younger men only make good
students.

--Tracy, 36

_____207.

The emotional release during sex is
more satisfying than the physical.

--Anne, 32

208._____

My husband still notices the little
things I do to please him.

--Tammy, 41

209._____

Real men know to be real gentle.

--Suzetta, 30

210._____

We use a hot, tasty lotion to get
things going.

--Janette, 34

_____

211.

We like to watch each other getting undressed. To me, that's part of foreplay.

--Belinda, 29

212.

I'm more careful today than ever before, and I only sleep with men who are just as careful.

--Helen, 41

213.

I like to be on top feeling him thrust up into me.

--Naomi, 28

214.

My inner thighs are super-sensitive.
Being kissed there makes me
squirm.

--Mary, 21

215.

If his eyes are on others, his hands
won't be on me.

--Mattie, 27

216.

I feel the most love from a man
during foreplay.

--Angelique, 31

217.

I think men use sex as an escape
from their everyday lives. I like it
to be a part of my mine.

--Josie, 34

218.

It's nice to lay my head on a man's
chest after we've made love,
listening to his heart pound.

--Lonnie, 27

219.

Before lovemaking, a little
pampering goes a long way.

--Sharon, 33

220.

I can't reach orgasm when I'm worried about something.

--Karen, 31

221.

I think men's orgasms are pretty much the same, but mine are always different.

--Gloria, 37

222.

I like to switch places.

--Pauline, 26

223.

Some nights I like to get real sleazy.
It's not always about love.

--Tamara, 35

224.

Don't pull out all the way during
sex. Air gets inside me and it's very
uncomfortable.

--Fran, 31

225.

My husband gets off on hearing
about what I did with other men
before we met. I wish I knew why.

--Meg, 32

226._____

It's important for me to not just
like a man, but to like myself when
I'm with him.

--Beverly, 35

227._____

Lick me from head to toe.

--Drenna, 26

228._____

I've got to have a variety of
positions.

--Elizabeth, 29

_____

229.

I rarely let a man ejaculate in my mouth, but no man will ever do that on my face. That's degrading.

--Kindra, 26

230.

Once you trust someone the sexually possibilities are unlimited.

--Cassie, 34

231.

I've got to have time for myself before I can give any time to a man.

--Hillery, 43

232._____

Stay away from my behind.

--Fiona, 23

233._____

I think men are so terrified of
failing in bed that they're afraid to
take any risks or to make themselves
vulnerable, which is a failure in
itself.

--Patty, 36

234._____

Intercourse in water is so soothing.

--Christa, 24

_____

235.

Wine is much more romantic than beer.

--Fay, 28

236.

Petting and necking like we were teenagers again is a great way to get me hot.

--Carla, 39

237.

I'm open to trying new things in bed as long as I don't feel pressured into it.

--Natalie, 29

238.

I faxed a nude picture of myself to my husband. I love this new technology.

--Lorin, 33

239.

Animal-lovers make wonderful lovers. There's a gentle quality about them.

--Marian, 38

240.

Reach for me even when we're not making love.

--Susan, 34

241.

I don't appreciate the jokes about how women smell like fish. To a real man, we smell like women.

--Lynn, 44

242.

My whole body is a sexual organ, not just my vagina.

--Ruth, 35

243.

I've never achieved orgasm through coitus. My lovers have to be willing to do more.

--Samantha, 42

244._____

If I feel that a man wants to take care of me, then I'm drawn to him sexually.

--Joline, 24

245._____

Sex is an animalistic desire. Love is displayed in other ways.

--Nicole, 38

246._____

I spend a lot of time making myself look attractive. I like a man who notices.

--Alison, 32

247.

Most men are into the same things --oral sex and the missionary position. Something off the beaten path would be a welcome change.

--Lina, 37

248.

Men always want to change positions too quickly.

--April, 32

249.

Nothing feels more natural than doing it in the woods like animals.

--Jacqueline, 28

250._____

He doesn't enter me until I tell
him. That way I always get enough
foreplay.

--Rebecca, 37

251._____

Men shouldn't view sex as a
conquest, but as an act of love.

--Deborah, 31

252._____

Looks aren't that important.
Women have five senses and sight
is only one of them.

--Melonie, 36

253.

Sex is only one part of the relationship. An important part, but just one part.

--Stephanie, 22

254.

I love to put my ankles on his shoulders and let the hair on the back of his head tickle my toes.

--Lindsay, 27

255.

I'd rather have great sex once a week than average sex every other day.

--Judy, 29

256._____

I really get off on the sound of our bellies slapping together.

--Cindy, 32

257._____

Contraception isn't only my responsibility.

--Julie, 31

258._____

When a man is finished, it doesn't mean I am.

--Tracey, 38

_____

259.

If I'm at a guy's place, he's got to have clean sheets on the bed or forget it.

--Katherine, 24

260.

I have to feel appreciated for who I am as a person first.

--Sophia, 37

261

Men should be more interested in satisfying their women instead of their egos.

--Peggy, 40

262.

Sex should be an act of affection, not aggression.

--Deidra, 29

263.

Every time doesn't have to be different. Theres something comforting in a routine.

--Laura, 33

264.

If we're in bed and the phone rings, just let it ring.

--Pheobe, 27

265.

Gentle kisses all over my body put me in the clouds.

--Megan, 23

266.

I like it when he slowly undresses me first--then himself.

--Janice, 26

267.

I don't like to guess at what makes a man feel good. I like for him to come right out and tell me.

--Cynthia, 21

268._____

Don't roll over and go to sleep. I'm
not your damn Sominex.

--Jaunita, 35

269._____

Sometimes we'll make a rule that
we can't talk at all in bed. We wind
up communicating in other ways.

--Mandy, 31

270._____

A soft body massage sets the perfect
mood.

--Carey, 34

_____

271.

Rub my legs, my back, all over
before you do me.

--Ellen, 33

272.

Bright lights in the bedroom make
me feel kind of self-conscious. I
like candlelight the best.

--Kristy, 30

273.

Making love standing up is very
erotic.

--Phyllis, 28

274.

The more he says my name, the more I'm into it.

--Evelyn, 28

275.

You've got to have a life outside of sex to make the relationship work.

--Paula, 32

276.

It's fun to put red bulbs in the bedroom lamps.

--Sheila, 36

277.

Please come to bed clean. I want to love you, not smell you.

--Justine, 31

278.

The lighter he touches me, the more I feel it.

--Dawn, 29

279.

My breasts are very special to me. A man has to treat them delicately.

--Deborah, 34

280._____

Strange places are the best.

--Clarice, 27

281._____

I've got two words on the subject--
whipped cream.

--Brittany, 32

282._____

I love it when he rubs my vagina
with the back of his hand.

--Vanessa, 37

_____

283.

I always feel funny about my body.
I like it when a man tells me how
beautiful and sexy he finds it.

--Daphne, 31

284.

Nothing should be allowed to
interrupt our lovemaking
--especially not the phone.

--Brittany, 24

285.

Oils and lotions do wonders for
your body and your sex.

--Trish, 27

286._____

Foot massages.

--Gracie, 34

287._____

Kiss my inner elbow.

--Allison, 28

288._____

The kitchen table is good for more
than dinner.

--Sheryl, 27

_____

289.

I think everyone should be a member of the Mile-High Club. I've initiated all of my boyfriends.

--Dena, 32

290.

Watch out for my hair when you're on top of me.

--Cassandra, 29

291.

Men should give more attention to the insides of my wrists.

--Bonnie, 27

292.

Be creative. Men and women have been having sex for millions of years, and there's a great deal more to do than the missionary position.

--Eva, 41

293.

About once a month we'll arrange a lunchtime encounter.

--Rosa, 39

294.

I love a man with strong, but gentle hands.

--Ophelia, 34

295.

I can tell a man is just looking for sex when he spends the whole night trying to get me drunk.

--Claudia, 25

296.

I like to be tickled. Not a lot, just a little.

--Beverly, 30

297.

There's no rule that says by the third date you should be in my pants. That's not the way it works.

--Lillian, 28

298.

I wish my husband would take the time to seduce me like he did before we were married.

--Ivy, 36

299.

My husband touches my face very softly during sex. That makes me feel special.

--Loretta, 34

300.

When I'm menstruating, intercourse is not pleasurable.

--Ruth, 30

_____**301.**

I love watching porno movies.
They come up with stuff I wouldn't
think of in a million years.

--Kathleen, 39

_____**302.**

Give me a couple of good buns to
grab hold of and I'm ready.

--Maria, 34

_____**303.**

I fantisize about doing it with a
total stranger, but in reality I have
to know the man well first.

--Bettie, 41

304._____

I don't want sex as often as he does,
and I'm glad he understands.

--Alana, 29

305._____

Treat my breasts with love.

--Angela, 33

306._____

The old bearskin rug is the best.

--Robyn, 26

_____

_____**307.**

I hate routine. I get enough of that
at work. I sure don't need it in my
bed.

--Rebecca, 36

_____**308.**

When we're together, nothing else
and nobody else should exist.

--Josephine, 31

_____**309.**

I have to feel like a woman before I
can make love. That means I have to
feel cherished and respected.

--Callie, 39

310._____

I can't resist having lotion rubbed all over my body.

--Karen, 26

311._____

Pets and children--outside.

--Danielle, 34

312._____

Cover me with little kisses all over my face and body.

--Shannon, 31

_____

313.

I get undressed to music, sort of a strip-tease. I think it gets me hotter than him.

--Patti, 33

314.

All the kissing and touching we do after sex is my favorite part.

--Bea, 44

315.

We draw a hot bath before we make love and then afterwards we just get in and soak in it.

--Stacy, 28

316._____

Just do it. I don't need all the
frills.

--Margery, 28

317._____

A little nibbling and kissing on my
earlobes tingles.

--Denise, 23

318._____

The less talking, the better.

--Kelly, 22

_____

319.

Oral sex is the only way my
husband can give me an orgasm.

--Robin, 34

320.

Dancing makes me feel like making
love. Good dancers usually make
good lovers.

--Paula, 23

321.

Mustaches tickle between my legs,
but beards just scratch.

--Roxanne, 28

322._____

Never stop trying new things in
bed.

--Diana, 35

323._____

No bodily contact at first. Use your
eyes to show me how you feel
about me.

--Erica, 34

324._____

I don't like to have my head pushed
and pulled when I'm giving oral
sex.

--Lynn, 32

_____

_____325.

When the actual sex begins, the kissing shouldn't end.

--Vivian, 30

_____326.

I like it when a guy uses his mouth on me, but I don't want anyone's fingers inside me.

--Sheila, 29

_____327.

Sometimes I'm just too tired. If my husband respects that, I'll make it up to him next time.

--Cheryl, 41

328._____

I love for him to keep saying my name.

--Lacy, 25

329._____

When I'm on top, I have much more control over how much of him is inside me and how fast we go. I like that feeling of power, though I'll never admit it to him.

--Andrea, 32

330._____

No headbanging music.

--Cyndi, 23

331.

Sex alone is an empty experience
for me. I have to feel something.

--Brooke, 24

332.

I like for him to share a secret
desire with me, then when we make
love I'll try to fulfill it.

--Connie, 32

333.

Most of the time, I masturbate
before sex in order to get myself in
the mood. But my husband can't
watch.

--Barbara, 40

334._____

It's fun in the shower when our bodies get all soaped up and slippery.

--Trish, 24

335._____

I wish my husband cared enough to ask me what I'd like.

--Gail, 29

336._____

Our lovemaking doesn't end with the orgasm.

--Evan, 30

337.

Music with a steady beat is great for establishing a good sexual rhythm.

--Candice, 38

338.

All women aren't turned on by the same things. Experiment and keep an open mind.

--Blair, 42

339.

During sex, there's a time to give and a time to take. And those times should be equally balanced.

--Lillian, 45

340._____

I need a chance to prepare myself for a sexual encounter. It can't be a spur-of-the-moment kind of thing.

--Cathy, 34

341._____

If it ain't broke, don't fix it. If it feels good, keep doing it.

--Dominique, 26

342._____

I can't enjoy it unless we're practicing safe sex.

--Maureen, 23

343.

I'm very shy, and I think most men take that to mean I'm not interested. I wish they'd take the time to get to know me.

--Marsha, 26

344.

Alchohol reduces my inhibitions. I only drink with a man I can trust.

--Susie, 29

345.

I had a boyfriend who used to let his dog watch us. No pets, please.

--Terri, 31

346._____

I like to talk about the sex right after we've had it. Likes and dislikes. You learn a lot about your lover that way.

--Jillian, 29

347._____

Tell me I turn you on.

--Forticia, 27

348._____

Men can separate their sex lives from their everyday life, but it's all one life to me.

--Madeline, 38

_____349.

My husband and I still hold hands.
Things like that are what keep our
sex lives happy and healthy.

--Louise, 46

_____350.

I love to smell myself on a man
after sex. It's the animal in me that
wants to claim him for myself.

--Juanita, 38

_____351.

You're only going to get out of it
what you're willing to put in.

--Sharon, 32

352._____

If he takes me to dinner, and then sits there and eats without saying a word, I know he's looking to get laid and nothing else.

--Dana, 24

353._____

Sex that isn't planned is the best sex on Earth.

--Karen, 23

354._____

Go slow--especially if we haven't done it in a while.

--Sandy, 32

355.

The skin under my breasts is very soft and sensitive. That's a place more men should know about.

--Alice, 31

356.

If a man takes the time to find out what I like, I'll always do the same.

--Jenny, 29

357.

When my husband's away on business, we'll get on the phone and masturbate together.

--Tonya, 35

358._____

Small, personal gifts let me know
he thinks I'm special.

--Tanya, 26

359._____

Oral sex in the tub with the shower
spraying down on us.

--Hollie, 22

360._____

If he kisses me on the inside of my
wrist I can feel my temperature
start to rise.

--Joyce, 30

_____

361.

I know it's half-time when my husband wants to do it. And he wonders why I just lay there.

--Vickie, 37

362.

Men always want to put it in before I'm ready. Wait until I'm wet.

--Elaine, 39

363.

My boyfriend and I act silly and cut up in bed. When it's about fun, the sex is always good.

--Christine, 25

364._____

I wish my husband took more pride
in his appearance. Would he care if
I didn't wash regularly?

--Leslie, 34

365._____

A little flick of the tongue around
my bikini line gives me
goosebumps.

--Kristin, 31

366._____

When I'm relaxed, I can enjoy sex.

--Faron, 25

_____**367.**

We come up with some very
interesting positions in our
recliner.

--Brenda, 34

_____**368.**

I have to see a man's eyes when he's
inside me.

--Wendy, 28

_____**369.**

I'm open to just about everything,
except anal sex.

--Dana, 24

_____

370._____

I like it when he holds my legs in the air by my ankles.

--Natasha, 28

371._____

Sex is empty without love.

--Becky, 24

372._____

If I tell a man he's hurting me, he'd better stop immediately.

--Rayanne, 33

_____

_____**373.**

I always crave sweets after I've had sex.

--Trisha, 30

_____**374.**

I did a threesome once with a guy and another girl. It's pretty wild to feel four hands and two mouths.

--Jolene, 33

_____**375.**

I know I shouldn't say this, but I like to lay back and let the man do all the work.

--Janice, 23

376._____

Play with my hair.

--Tonnie, 24

377._____

I love it when he gives me oral sex while he's completely under the covers.

--Charlene, 27

378._____

We'll watch porno videos and not touch each other. Then we'll turn them off and get down to business.

--Ashley, 29

379.

I can tell he's going to be a good lover if he knows exactly how to unhook my bra.

--Carmin, 34

380.

Why are men so eager to have an orgasm? When they do, the fun is usually over.

--Graci, 39

381.

I love it when my boyfriend kneads my butt while we're doing it.

--Tori, 27

382._____

When he's going down on me, I like
hearing those wet, slurping noises.

--Janet, 34

383._____

It's all in the way he touches me
--softly and with tenderness.

--Sue, 36

384._____

I get turned on when we're French
kissing and he licks my teeth.

--Julia, 26

_____

385.

If we're at a restaurant, I like to play under the table while we look perfectly respectable from above.

--Glenda, 38

386.

I can derive pleasure from just about any part of my body.

--Lynn, 26

387.

Condoms are cold when a man first puts one on. He should let it warm up a minute before he puts it in.

--Natalie, 29

388._____

Kiss me all over.

--Donna, 28

389._____

If a man has satin sheets, I can't wait
to get naked.

--Sherri, 26

390._____

Kisses on the back of my neck get
me horny.

--Colette, 31

_____

391.

I've always felt that if you don't break a sweat, you're not doing it right.

--Pauline, 22

392.

My ideal lovemaking session is Sunday morning in bed with strawberries and cream making slow, soft love.

--Amber, 30

393.

Feeling loved makes me feel sexy.

--Marie, 33

394.

The one time I told my husband about a fantasy, he laughed. I've never told him another one.

--Gwendolyn, 23

395.

My breasts are so sensitive during my period that nothing feels good.

--Michelle, 32

396.

Guys expect me to worship their penises just because I don't have one. Give me a break.

--Maria, 35

397.

Short guys try harder in bed.

--Holly, 27

398.

Some men make me feel like I'm a receptacle for their anger. Those are the ones I avoid.

--Kay, 34

399.

The bigger, the better. I like for a man to completely fill me up inside.

--Maureen, 38

400._____

I can't enjoy receiving oral sex if
the man has not shaved.

--Felicia, 26

401._____

I love knowing that my husband has
told his friends what I do to him. I
hope they're jealous as hell.

--Sulia, 28

402._____

It's not where you are or what
you're doing, it's who you're with.

--Beth, 32

_____

403.

Sex shouldn't be confined to the bedroom. It shouldn't even be confined to the house.

--Mindy, 33

404.

Every now and then, it's good to put your love for your partner aside and let lust take over.

--Erica, 39

405.

We do it once for him, then again for me.

--Amie, 32

406._____

If I'll never see you again, forget it.

--Constance, 32

407._____

I like lazy sex. I want to take my time and enjoy it.

--Patricia, 36

408._____

Even if a man has a great job, I don't want to talk about it all the time.

--Lorraine, 31

409.

What a man can do for me physically isn't as important as how he makes me feel on the inside.

--Joanna, 35

410.

I don't like to get naked all at once. I reveal my body to him in stages.

--Simone, 41

411.

Opening lines are fun to hear, but I don't take the man who uses them seriously.

--Kimberly, 28

412._____

Explore every inch of me with
your tongue.

--Cheryl, 29

413._____

Tell me what you're thinking while
we're in the act.

--Julie, 26

414._____

Save it all up for the weekend.

--Alyce, 31

_____

_____**415.**

Having my hair brushed feels
indescribably wonderful.

--Blair, 23

_____**416.**

Small, thoughtful gifts mean more
to me. If a gift is too expensive, I
can't help feeling pressured.

--Paige, 28

_____**417.**

Reaching orgasm simultaneously is
the ultimate feeling of
togetherness.

--Randi, 25

418._____

Movie stars are fun to fantasize about, but I want a real man.

--Melissa, 24

419._____

We're a team outside of the bedroom, and that makes the sex superb.

--Donna, 29

420._____

If a man can't sit and talk for a while, why does he think I'll sleep with him?

--Annette, 32

421.

Men who have traveled and had some life experience are always more passionate lovers.

--Aileen, 44

422.

I think I probably look pretty disgusting when I'm on top. I feel better when he tells me I'm pretty.

--Leanne, 23

423.

If a guy's divorced, I really don't want to hear about his ex-wife.

--Melinda, 34

424.

A clean-smelling man gets me hot.

--Sharon, 26

425.

I'm a sucker for a man in uniform.

--Kimberli, 31

426.

Atmosphere: candles, potpourri, soft music.

--Nancy, 34

427.

I'm all for spontaneity, but I do need time to put my diaphram in.

--Nadine, 30

428.

Rock or rap doesn't get it when it's time to make love. Something slower and more natural is the ticket.

--Nona, 28

429.

I wish most men knew what their breath really smells like.

--Monica, 31

430.

I think I've heard all the opening lines. Men should invent some new ones.

--Lillie, 33

431.

I have a low self-image. I need constant reassurance that he finds me desirable.

--Suzanne, 24

432.

He appreciates the job I do around the house, and I appreciate that.

--Ellen, 28

433.

All the women I've ever known, including myself, take Valentine's Day much more seriously than men.

--Diane, 36

434.

Men say more with a look than they'll ever realize.

--Naomi, 34

435.

When I see a new man my eyes head straight for his butt.

--Sally, 22

436._____

He takes my hand, kisses it, and leads me into the bedroom. How's that for romantic?

--Sandra, 34

437._____

Men shouldn't wear too much cologne.

--Barbera, 31

438._____

A man who can play music is always a wonderful lover.

--Kerra, 25

439.

I don't like to undress myself. That should be his job.

--Jo Ann, 32

440.

My fondest sexual memory is when we did it outside in the pouring rain.

--Gloria, 36

441.

Don't put your clothes on right afterwards. I can go the whole weekend without getting dressed.

--Jessica, 29

442.

Don't rush me.

--Rosa Lee, 22

443.

I love to be undressed like a little girl.

--Pamela, 26

444.

If you've been together for some time, you should take a weekend to get reacquainted.

--Whitney, 32

_____

445.

Once a man has discovered how to get me off, he stops exploring. There is more than one way.

--Angela, 38

446.

Love is the world's most potent aphrodisiac--not power.

--Taylor, 31

447.

Female orgasms come in all different sizes and intensities.

--Belinda, 35

448._____

We show each other what we'd like
done to ourselves.

--Stacey, 30

449._____

Tell me your hopes and dreams and
how I play a part in them.

--Jeanie, 25

450._____

We do it on my imitation fur coat.

--Lynise, 23

_____

451.

I feel sexier and less inhibited in the dark.

--Pam, 27

452.

Some of the best sex I've ever had didn't involve intercourse.

--Paulette, 26

453.

If men learned how to be themselves, they'd get laid a hell of a lot more often.

--Julia, 38

454._____

If we can laugh at ourselves, we can love each other.

--Sherry, 37

455._____

I've got to trust him before I can let go and experience great sex.

--Sonya, 33

456._____

Making love is best on a cold, wet, windy night.

--Vanessa, 28

_____

457.

Smells turn me on. Scented candles or incense make all the difference to me when it's time for sex.

--Lea, 24

458.

By the time we're finished, there isn't an inch of our bodies we haven't touched.

--Becca, 27

459.

Start soft and then get harder, not the other way around.

--Glenn, 31

460._____

If a man gets into my bed, he's going to stay the night.

--Ann, 26

461._____

I enjoy it when he kisses and caresses my tummy, just beneath my navel.

--Gloria, 32

462._____

I need a relationship before I crawl into bed.

--Stephanie, 31

_____

463.

I never get too much foreplay.

--Rhonda, 36

464.

Monogamy, to me, means worry
-free sex.

--Bailey, 24

465.

The sweetest lover I ever had would
always bring me a cool, damp
washcloth when we were finished.

--Virginia, 48

466.

Foreplay is supposed to be fun. If it wasn't, they would have called it "forework."

--Blair, 30

467.

Tell me I'm pretty.

--Mollie, 24

468.

My boyfriend always makes sure I have my first orgasm before he even puts it in.

--Tina, 28

469.

Afterwards, I like to sit on my boyfriend's lap like a little girl.

--Lisa, 22

470.

I get all hot and bothered when my boyfriend whispers what he'd like me to do to him.

--Kelsey, 26

471.

Men should learn the art of "the tease."

--Molly, 34

472._____

It's not just sex, it's an adventure.

--Sybil, 27

473._____

I want a man who makes love and means it.

--Joyce, 29

474._____

I love it when we get all hot and sweaty.

--Susan, 23

_____

_____475.

Sex is an animalistic urge. I need to
be shown love in other ways.

--Debra, 39

_____476.

I can let myself go with the man
I'm with now because I know he'll
still respect me afterwards.

--Sandra, 32

_____477.

Once, my husband came to my
office, flashed me, then left. I
couldn't wait to get home.

--Beverly, 38

478._____

A man who takes pleasure in my orgasms is the only kind of man for me.

--Crystal, 34

479._____

I'm a big girl. I want a big man.

--Lisa, 31

480._____

I like to hold his testicles in my hand. They're so warm and soft.

--Nora, 26

_____

_____**481.**

I've never been stirred up into such a sexual frenzy that I would do it without a condom.

--Joyce, 28

_____**482.**

If I'm giving you oral sex, don't force yourself into my mouth.

--Dusty, 25

_____**483.**

I don't think women can turn it on and turn it off as easily as men can. I need more time on both ends.

--Lori, 23

484.

I was raised that premarital sex was bad. I do it, but sometimes I feel guilty.

--Vickie, 21

485.

No burping or farting in bed.

--Linda, 28

486.

Anyplace where there's a chance of getting caught.

--Tequita, 30

487.

When a man asks me to leave my shoes on I feel like he wants me to be his whore; I'm insulted.

--Trisha, 27

488.

Chinese food tastes best after sex.

--Amanda, 34

489.

Soft moans are what I listen for when I'm wondering if something feels good to him.

--Janie, 32

490._____

We each say one word in turn until
we've formed a sentence. Then we
do what we've created.

--Jean, 26

491._____

I like men who aren't afraid of their
feelings.

--Winnie, 25

492._____

Old music from the 20's and 30's is
great sex music.

--Sylvia, 31

493.

Once you sleep with a friend, you can never go back to being just that.

--Becky, 39

494.

I hate it when a man asks me where I learned something in bed. It's none of his business.

--Emma, 31

495.

Great foreplay makes for even greater sex.

--Marleen, 34

496._____

A man doesn't have to be the handsomest guy in the room, he just has to be interesting.

--Olivia, 31

497._____

I've got just as much to offer outside of the bedroom. I want a man who knows it.

--Grace, 36

498._____

We always start out with me on top. That way I can ease him into me.

--Muriel, 34

499.

When a man reaches orgasm before me, he'd better know his job is only half-finished.

--Karlotta, 33

500.

No talking. Just the sound of our bodies together.

--Stacey, 38

501.

When he takes his finger and gently rubs my clitoris while he's inside me--instant orgasm.

--Gail, 41

502._____

The way to a man's heart is through
his penis. Sad, but true.

--Kara, 34

503._____

I can't trust a man who turns into a
different person when he drinks.

--Christina, 30

504._____

My husband gives me oral sex with
a menthol cough drop in his mouth.

--Justine, 29

_____

_____**505.**

I only have an orgasm when I'm
relaxed. When it's obvious a guy's
trying too hard, I'm not relaxed.

--Haley, 34

_____**506.**

I'm gonna put a traffic sign over my
bed that says, "Slow Down."

--Sonya, 38

_____**507.**

When you kiss me, don't use your
tongue like you're unclogging a
drain.

--Rosa, 27

_____

508._____

Bathing together is fantastic. The tub can be sexier than the bed.

--Kalen, 25

509._____

Intimacy means sharing your feelings, not your bodily fluids.

--Nancy, 31

510._____

Cologne tastes awful. Don't put any where I might kiss you.

--Shannon, 28

_____**511.**

When I'm made to feel special is
when I feel sexiest.

--Jeanne, 32

_____**512.**

Never ask me what other men do.
I'm with you--do what you do.

--Katie, 30

_____**513.**

Touch me all over, don't just grab at
the obvious.

--Arlene, 28

_____

514.

Most women are romantics, but there are some of us who aren't. We just want to get laid and leave.

--Laura, 32

515.

Guys might get aroused quickly, but it takes girls longer.

--Brittany, 26

516.

The before and after parts of sex are more fun than the during.

--Samantha, 29

517.

Climaxing at the same time is great when it happens, but you shouldn't worry if it doesn't.

--Corine, 35

518.

I've never had a man who's given me enough foreplay.

--Anita, 41

519.

Remember the scene with the ice cube in *9 1/2 Weeks*? Try it, you'll like it.

--Veronica, 23

520._____

It's really wild to watch yourself
do it on video.

--Taylor, 22

521._____

I want him to kiss me all over my
neck and face.

--Kelsey, 31

522._____

Go slow and let the feelings inside
me build.

--June, 35

_____

523.

I like him to bring home sexy
nighties and lingerie. I like
wearing things I know he likes.

--Raquel, 31

524.

Every so often my boyfriend will
call me at work and tell me what he
wants to do to me. I love that.

--Melonie, 26

525.

Leave on the lights. I want to watch.

--Jackie, 25

526.

I like how a man tastes right after he's come out of a swimming pool.

--Stacey, 26

527.

I have to be sure he's my friend before anything else.

--Theresa, 28

528.

We do it on our patio under the stars, and my husband shows me his Big Dipper.

--Karen, 33

529.

I love to lay in the tub and let him wash me all over--even shave my legs.

--Corina, 32

530.

I don't want to have sex with a man who smells or hasn't shaved.

--Bev, 28

531.

A man who touches me just for the sake of touching me is my favorite.

--Pamela, 35

532.

I don't like blurting out instructions. If a man asks, though, I'll tell him.

--Candice, 31

533.

Gentle most of the time. Every once in a while can be rough.

--Cheryl, 24

534.

Men that are super-serious in bed turn me off. It's supposed to be fun.

--Leanne, 23

_____**535.**

The sexiest thing my husband does
is sing to me.

--Tonya, 32

_____**536.**

Some men act like they can't wait
for it to be over. I like men who
want to make it last.

--Sue, 37

_____**537.**

Let's pretend and play different
roles.

--Judith, 33

_____

538._____

Fear of somebody discovering us adds to the intensity.

--Joanna, 28

539._____

Making love in the car makes me feel like a high-school girl again. Of course, now I prefer a much roomier car.

--Helen, 35

540._____

I have these colored markers, and we draw on each other's bodies.

--Venessa, 26

541.

Trains are very romantic and sexy.

--Ellen, 38

542.

It's fun to act out fantasies we've seen in the movies.

--Monique, 29

543.

My husband gets pretty sweaty at work. I'm thankful he's considerate enough to shower before we do it.

--Shannon, 34

544._____

Earlier is better. When I'm ready
for bed, I'm ready to sleep.

--Lola, 31

545._____

Satin sheets and I'm in heaven.

--Gorgette, 34

546._____

A clean-shaven face is quite sexy.
Stubble stings.

--Madeline, 30

_____

547.

I like to talk before, during and after intercourse.

--Toni, 36

548.

There are lots of men who think we're obligated to have sex with them because they've bought us a few drinks. They've got another thing coming.

--Shelly, 33

549.

Do it hard when we're doggie-style.

--Leslie, 26

550._____

I refuse to let a man spend money on me. I don't want to feel obligated when he starts making advances.

--Sabrina, 26

551._____

My husband still wants to do it when I've got my period. I think he'd do it with me if I were dead.

--Clara, 35

552._____

Twice in one day is rare, and nice.

--Barbara, 38

553.

Flowers are cliche, I know, but they still do the trick for me.

--Brandy, 27

554.

Please come to bed clean.

--Pam, 34

555.

The first thing I check out on a man is his butt. Then I work my way around to the other side.

--Corrie, 29

556._____

He's got to like himself before I
can.

--Linda, 33

557._____

Sex is an act of love, not of
vengeance.

--Camille, 32

558._____

I get off on doing it in other
people's houses. Like at a party, or
if I'm house-sitting for a friend.

--Nicole, 31

_____

_____**559.**

I don't want to do it when I'm
indisposed.

--*Chelsea, 22*

_____**560.**

A man has got to use his
imagination to keep me interested
sexually. I like to try new things.

--*Colene, 28*

_____**561.**

Good sex begins with a good time.
I'm always up for ice cream.

--*Sally, 23*

562._____

Safe sex is an absolute must.

--Judy, 29

563._____

Little kisses and strokes on the
insides of my thighs feel glorious.

--Niki, 24

564._____

Strobe lights are awesome.

--Corine, 21

_____

_____565.

Guys shouldn't confuse love and
lust--not in their partners, and not
in themselves.

--Valerie, 30

_____566.

The more wine, the better. I tend to
be a bit uptight otherwise.

--Kim, 29

_____567.

Men always get so nervous after
we're done. It's like I'm going to
rate them. Just enjoy it.

--Robin, 28

568.

As long as there's romance, there will be good sex.

--Lillian, 38

569.

On a cold night in front of a hot fire is the best.

--Sheila, 31

570.

If it gets back to me that a guy has bragged to his friends about us sleeping together, it's over.

--Carol Ann, 25

_____571.

We like to take turns massaging each other all over.

--Rene, 27

_____572.

I will never sleep with a man on the first or second date. It sets a bad precedent for the entire relationship.

--Glenda, 33

_____573.

I shouldn't be expected to supply the condoms.

--Mary, 23

574.

Ease into it with plenty of foreplay.

--Paige, 31

575.

Intercourse is one thing; oral sex is only for someone special.

--Vicki, 23

576.

If he won't take the time to get to know me, I'm not interested in sex.

--Sherry, 24

577.

I wish men would stop trying to find my G-spot.

--June, 31

578.

Lunchtime rendezvous are oh, so romantic.

--Kelly, 34

579.

Make love to me with your body and not some plastic, vibrating toy.

--Penelope, 41

580._____

Doggie-style makes me feel used.

--Linda, 25

581._____

He shouldn't call it "knocking
bumps," "doing the nasty" or any of
that other stuff.

--Felicia, 24

582._____

I'm not into being another notch in
his bedpost.

--Kelly, 28

_____

583.

Let me initiate sex sometimes, too.

--Lydia, 35

584.

My advice to men can be summed up in the song title, "Try a Little Tenderness."

--Nan, 43

585.

Don't talk about work while we're having sex.

--Bonnie, 32

586._____

Variety is the spice of my sex life.

--Sharon, 30

587._____

Actions speak louder than words,
especially in matters of the heart.

--Julie, 33

588._____

If you believe I'm beautiful, then I
am.

--Margaret, 36

_____

589.

The only time he's affectionate is
when he's horny. I wish there
weren't always strings attached.

--Darian, 26

590.

I like it when he watches me take
my clothes off.

--Barb, 29

591.

My whole body is an erogenous
zone.

--Millie, 31

592._____

I'm usually not that wet when a man first enters me. Short in-and-out thrusts help me take it all.

--Denise, 35

593._____

No TV while we're doing it.

--Lisa, 36

594._____

Lovemaking doesn't begin and end with his penis inside me.

--Valerie, 26

595.

More foreplay would be wonderful.

--Kim, 37

596.

Sexy gifts, like lingerie, make me feel very special.

--Vivian, 42

597.

I want to be appreciated for *me*, not just my body.

--Adrienne, 21

598.

Marshmallow fluff goes good with a man.

--Patricia, 31

599.

No outside noise, only the sound of our bodies.

--Simone, 25

600.

Silly, romantic, old movies do something for me sexually.

--Selena, 34

601.

I love feeling the sunlight on my body while we're having sex.

--Elaine, 31

602.

Sex more than twice a week can get a bit tiresome.

--Beverly, 35

603.

If a man has a lot of pubic hair, he should trim some of it off.

--Diane, 41

604._____

Try it in a hammock. It takes
coordination.

--Hanna, 26

605._____

When I'm tired, sex is the last thing
on my mind.

--Liz, 32

606._____

I put my legs together and he
massages them until they just fall
open.

--Didi, 28

_____

607.

There are other things in life
besides an orgasm.

--Jill, 31

608.

My boyfriend hums when he's
giving me oral sex. The vibration
drives me crazy.

--Linda, 26

609.

Wear boxers, not jockeys.

--Ruth, 32

610._____

We write dirty notes to each other
and leave them where we know the
other will find them.

--Brenda, 28

611._____

I've purposely left the windows
open so people could hear us.

--Kimberly, 31

612._____

We have a beautiful bedroom, but
sometimes it's fun to check into a
motel.

--Annie, 36

613.

Sometimes I'll go to a bar and my husband will come in and "pick me up." It's like we're single again.

--Regina, 38

614.

When my boyfriend tells me I look like an angel, I'm ready to prove him wrong.

--Susan, 23

615.

I'll only share my fantasies with a man who can keep a secret.

--Denise, 29

616.

Tattoos are a turn off.

--Wendy, 32

617.

I can't have great sex if there's a chance I might get pregnant.

--Jan, 22

618.

I like the missionary position, except I put my feet on his chest.

--Marie, 28

_____**619.**

If a man is with me, I expect his full attention.

--Helen, 32

_____**620.**

I like standing up with the man on his knees giving me oral sex.

--Nina, 26

_____**621.**

Never when I'm on my period.

--Tracie, 23

_____

622.

I like it when you're so familiar
with your partner that a look says it
all.

--Carrie, 38

623.

Kisses on my cleavage are sweet.

--Paula, 27

624.

I love it when he holds my breasts
while we do it.

--Jackie, 23

625.

I don't like my anus touched at all. Anywhere but there.

--Nancy, 34

626.

Bikini briefs don't do anything for most men.

--Eilene, 28

627.

I've dated guys who get so drunk they can't even get it up. Men should know their limit.

--Wanda, 31

628._____

When I give oral sex, I don't like
for him to watch me.

--Allison, 29

629._____

I love to make love by candlelight.

--Dawn, 34

630._____

Edible panties and novelty sex toys
are a lot of fun.

--Karen, 26

_____

————————————————631.

My husband lets me bathe him, and that excites us both.

--Phyllis, 36

————————————————632.

My favorite thing is when my boyfriend kneels down, slides my panties off and kisses the inside of my thighs.

--Yvonne, 33

————————————————633.

Touch my face and look into my eyes.

--Darla, 28

634._____

Don't let previous lovers hinder your making love to me.

--Irene, 38

635._____

I love soft kisses on my eyelids.

--Amanda, 28

636._____

Touch my breasts gently.

--Melissa, 22

_____

637.

I sit in this overstuffed chair and throw my legs over each arm. There's no end to the ways he can satisfy me like that.

--Natalie, 37

638.

A good back massage is the best foreplay.

--Terry, 31

639.

I don't do anything without a condom--even oral sex.

--Julie, 28

640._____

I like my boyfriend to shave my
bikini line.

--Diana, 24

641._____

Hickies are for kids.

--Michelle, 27

642._____

We love to get under a big down
comforter and get nasty.

--Kay, 32

643.

Start at my toes and kiss your way up to my nose.

--Sharon, 21

644.

Role reversal can spice things up.

--Fran, 34

645.

My husband looks at me like I'm the most beautiful girl in the world. That's better than an orgasm.

--Melinda, 31

646.

Don't start paying attention to me only when you want sex.

--Tina, 29

647.

I like it when he puts his head in my lap.

--Maureen, 33

648.

I need manual stimulation during intercourse to reach orgasm.

--Jill, 30

_____**649.**

It's how a man uses his penis, not
how big it is.

--Denise, 41

_____**650.**

I like my husband to pick out what I
wear to bed.

--Amy, 31

_____**651.**

Sometimes air gets trapped in my
vagina. That's not a good feeling.

--Tanya, 27

_____

652.

I wouldn't love my husband any less, or enjoy sex any less, if his penis were any smaller.

--Rachel, 41

653.

Lovemaking should be reserved for lovers only.

--Bonnie, 31

654.

I like to feel his tongue dancing around my body.

--Ursula, 37

655.

Sex should be fun and carefree. If you know it's not going to feel that way, then it's not the right time yet. Be patient.

--Rosalind, 34

656.

I have to be told that I have a sexy body.

--Mandy, 31

657.

Let go. Don't be so serious.

--Paula, 29

658.

When you think we've had enough foreplay, do it ten minutes longer.

--Tammy, 29

659.

I know I can be a bitch sometimes, and I like being with a man who doesn't let me get away with it.

--Donna, 27

660.

Part of what makes sex so great is that you're living for the moment. Try it outside of sex, too.

--Anna, 39

661.

When I tell a man how much I enjoyed the evening, it's not an invitation to sleep over.

--Shawnee, 27

662.

I want to be pampered--not jumped.

--Cheri, 31

663.

If he asks me my sign, he's going home alone.

--Laurie, 34

664.

I can't respect a guy who doesn't respect my cat.

--Sally, 33

665.

Make me feel like I'm your one and only.

--Darlene, 28

666.

Don't be afraid to ask if you're doing it right. If you're doing it wrong, you might not get another chance.

--Gina, 31

667.

Give me a chance to come, too.

--Trudy, 31

668.

I wish I could invite a man into my apartment without him assuming I want sex.

--Bea, 37

669.

Listen to what I'm saying with my body. It speaks the universal language.

--Jessica, 22

670._____

Indecision is a bad quality in a man.
If he's not sure what he wants, he's
probably not sure if he wants me.

--Karen, 40

671._____

No tongues until I kiss you with my
lips apart.

--Janet, 26

672._____

I like for the bed to be high off the
ground so it's like an alter, or a
stage.

--Morgan, 39

_____

673.

I work just as hard as any man, and I like to be treated with the same amount of dignity.

--Dannielle, 33

674.

Give me a man who knows how to moan.

--Melissa, 26

675.

I enjoy hearing about his kids, but they don't help me get in the mood.

--Betty, 43

676._____

Men shouldn't be so nervous. A calm man is a confident man, and confidence is a turn on.

--Susanna, 32

677._____

I like to put the condom on him.

--Belinda, 24

678._____

Curiousity is a powerful aphrodisiac.

--Dianne, 31

679.

I don't want to hear about any of your other experiences when we're having sex.

--Teri, 32

680.

When a man cops a cheap feel, I lose all respect for him.

--Pauline, 25

681.

A romantic night of dinner, dancing and drinks is a great way to start the evening.

--Nina, 33

682._____

I work hard and spend a great deal of
money in order to look good for
you. Please take the time to notice.

--Pam, 33

683._____

The honeymoon isn't over until
you decide it is.

--Rebecca, 35

684._____

He has to be comfortable touching
and being touched.

--Linda, 26

685.

My boyfriend shows me he loves me with little surprises.

--Karen, 23

686.

Macho types are definitely a turn off.

--Virginia, 27

687.

Clothes are expensive. Don't rip them off me like they're rags.

--Kelly, 26

688.

I enjoy getting compliments even if I don't always think they're sincere.

--Becky, 36

689.

He's got to take pride in his appearance.

--Janice, 34

690.

When I'm naked, I appreciate it if he takes a moment to enjoy the view before jumping on top of me.

--Dana, 28

691.

Women don't all need the same things. Find out what my special needs are, then fill them.

--Delores, 33

692.

I want the room ice cold so we can snuggle together under the comforter.

--Jan, 28

693.

I like a true gentleman--one who'll open doors and treat me like a lady.

--Hillary, 37

694._____

It's always worth it to wait awhile
and let our imaginations run wild.

--Yvette, 31

695._____

Most men do all the same stuff, all
the same way. Have something that
only *you* do in bed and be unique.

--Frieda, 42

696._____

Lift my skirt up very, very slowly.

--Sarah, 24

_____

697.

I'm into intense and powerful lovemaking. Strength gets me off.

--Jane, 31

698.

Clean sheets and bed linens are a must.

--Misty, 23

699.

My sex drive changes with the events in my life.

--Linnie, 25

700._____

Sexual technique is more important to older men, and I love them for it.

--Teresa, 28

701._____

When you start making up rules in the bedroom, you place needless limitations on your sexual experiences.

--Marshelle, 29

702._____

If he's good in the kitchen, he's good in the bedroom.

--Carla, 37

_____**703.**

Sex in the morning is great. Afterwards, we read the paper and share some hot chocolate.

--Helen, 34

_____**704.**

I want affection all the time, not just during intercourse.

--Dana, 23

_____**705.**

Play acting is fine once we feel secure with each other.

--Lisa, 26

_____

706._____

If you've ever slept with another man, you owe it to me to tell me about it.

--Arlene, 30

707._____

I only blush around men I'm attracted to.

--Sheri, 25

708._____

I like to go dancing with a new man. That way I can see how it feels to have him touch me.

--Deidre, 32

_____**709.**

Good food and good conversation
stimulate me.

--Trinity, 24

_____**710.**

I like sweet kisses all over my face
and neck.

--Linda, 22

_____**711.**

Flirt with me and I'll never get
bored.

--Angela, 38

_____

712._____

I like positions where I can see him
going inside me.

--Karen, 25

713._____

Whenever I have a man as a friend, I
always wind up sleeping with him.
I'm too curious for my own good.

--Fay, 33

714._____

One time, he put flower petals all
over the bed and we made the best
love ever on top of them.

--Carmen, 26

_____

715.

You shouldn't be able to tell where the foreplay ends and the actual sex begins.

--Patrice, 35

716.

When the novelty wears off, creativity takes over.

--Jasmine, 33

717.

My husband keeps going after he's had his orgasm until I've had mine. I love him for that.

--Debrecia, 30

718.

The closer we are in our minds, the better the sex.

--Kathy, 24

719.

Loyalty is the key to relationships, including sexual ones.

--Monica, 36

720.

There's nothing like an all-over tongue-bath.

--Erica, 29

721.

After lovemaking, we lay around naked talking until all hours.

--Cristine, 26

722.

I love it when he takes off my bra and then kisses my shoulders where the straps were.

--Renee, 28

723.

Men need to take it slower.

--Lora, 21

724.

I like the same type of music and man in bed--hard, steady and pounding.

--Fiona, 25

725.

Tell me what you're going to do to me as you strip me naked.

--Kristy, 27

726.

I feel sexy and pretty when he surrounds me with sexy and pretty things.

--Linda, 32

727.

Sometimes we'll pretend we're wild animals stalking each other.

--Ashley, 27

728.

Sex should be shared, not some sort of payback.

--Karen, 23

729.

The "dance" leading up to sex is always the mind-set factor for me.

--Maralyn, 22

730.＿＿＿＿＿＿＿＿＿＿＿

His eyes say it all.

--Lisa, 32

731.＿＿＿＿＿＿＿＿＿＿＿

I don't regret sleeping with men I wasn't in love with. But now that I know the difference, I'd never do it again.

--Leslie, 38

732.＿＿＿＿＿＿＿＿＿＿＿

As children, men weren't taught to take pleasure in *giving* pleasure, and it shows in their sexual apathy.

--Joyce, 39

_____**733.**

I wish there were more men who could sweep me off my feet. I like to be overwhelmed.

--Josette, 39

_____**734.**

Seeing other animals mate makes me want to. We watch PBS often.

--Faye, 32

_____**735.**

Lay back and let me work my magic. Don't worry about saying or doing the right things.

--Sylvia, 40

736._____

Many an intimate, loving evening
has been ruined by sex.

--Franchesca, 37

737._____

Hold me like you'll never let me
go.

--Beverly, 31

738._____

I'm a vegetarian, but not when it
comes to sex. Nibbling on a man is
sexy and exhilarating.

--Clair, 28

_____**739.**

The best sex I ever had didn't
involve any nudity.

--*Claudia, 24*

_____**740.**

Dance for me. Put on a show and
I'll stuff dollars into your shorts.

--*Shanon, 31*

_____**741.**

Help me with things around the
house and I'll make it worth your
while.

--*Allanda, 33*

_____

742.

Men think we can't see them staring at us, but we can. And no matter what we might say, we like it.

--Chelsea, 28

743.

A variety of sexual positions keeps our love-life interesting.

--Jean, 43

744.

If men played "hard to get" a little more, they'd be that much more desirable.

--Chea, 34

_____**745.**

When you come to bed, don't forget to bring the romance.

--Leila, 36

_____**746.**

I feel like sex is more for the man's benefit, but the foreplay is for me.

--Sue, 34

_____**747.**

Give me foreplay or give me death.

--Trisha, 28

748._____

My sexuality is my most prized
possession. You have to be
someone special for me to share it.

--Heather, 29

749._____,_____

The men I respect most are the ones
who realize that they can always
learn something new about women.

--Cicily, 36

750._____

We still go to the drive-in to make
out.

--Bette, 38

751.

I prefer a man who isn't afraid to tell me what he wants in bed.

--Liz, 34

752.

The perfect sex for me is an hour of foreplay, thirty minutes of hard intercourse, then snuggling the rest of the night.

--Theresa, 41

753.

When he does oral sex, he turns his head sideways.

--Josie, 31

754._____

Only saying, "I love you," during sex isn't enough.

--Ginger, 40

755._____

When my husband washes my hair, I can feel all the tension leave my body. I'm ready for sex after that.

--Stefanie, 31

756._____

The more you give, the more you get.

--Danielle, 27

757.

I love to put an old sheet on the bed
and break out the finger-paint.

--Gena, 28

758.

Biting is okay.

--Jennifer, 26

759.

Don't make your kisses too wet.
I'm not a sponge.

--Vivian, 31

760.

Candles in the bedroom provide a magnificent atmosphere for making love.

--Trish, 32

761.

If I walked up to a male stranger and said, "Let's go to bed," he'd do it. It doesn't work that way with women.

--Kelly, 34

762.

I only sleep with men who realize pleasure is a two-way street.

--Julie, 26

763.

The things a man does every day influence my feelings towards him more than his performance in the bedroom.

--Tina, 31

764.

It's fun to play cards, and the winner gets to pick whatever sexual treat they want.

--Melissa, 26

765.

Laughter is sexy.

--Megan, 29

766.

It seems to make most guys uncomfortable, but I like it when a man lets me undress him.

--Toni, 35

767.

Some wine or champagne puts me in a sexual frame of mind.

--Sylvia, 39

768.

Men equate laughter in bed as laughter aimed at them, but it's really a sign of a good time.

--Ariel, 28

769.

I love silk or satin against my bare skin.

--Janis, 27

770.

Show me you love me even when we're not making love.

--Rita, 24

771.

I like being tied up. But only if I can tie him up next time.

--Tamie, 33

772._____

I love the sounds he makes when I'm going down on him. If he didn't make those sounds, I wouldn't do it as often.

--Maralyn, 36

773._____

Having the backs of my knees kissed doesn't sound pleasurable, but it is.

--Tami, 23

774._____

I like to pretend I'm a hooker and he's my john.

--Daphne, 27

_____**775.**

Never leave your socks on, no
matter how cold it is.

--Sondra, 37

_____**776.**

Knead my butt like you're making
bread.

--Robin, 30

_____**777.**

Make sure the lights are low. I look
better that way.

--Elizabeth, 32

778._____

I like listening to Jazz during sex.
It seems so out of control, but it's
really not. That's how I like my
lovemaking to be, too.

--Catherine, 33

779._____

The more he wants to please me, the
more I want to please him.

--Yvette, 25

780._____

I like to remain perfectly still right
after I've had an orgasm and savor it.

--Yvonne, 31

_____**781.**

We like to take a sleeping bag
outside and zip ourselves up in it.

--Diane, 34

_____**782.**

Sex, off and on, all night long is
wonderful.

--Saundra, 28

_____**783.**

I'll never let a man use sex to take
out his anger and frustrations.

--Brigette, 35

784._____

Don't assume I'm using protection.

--Amy, 26

785._____

Nibble on my earlobes.

--Dale, 33

786._____

Don't bring up another girl in bed.

--Mimi, 29

_____

_____**787.**

I love it when he calls out my
name.

--Donna, 30

_____**788.**

We enjoy renting an X-rated video
and imitating what they do on the
screen.

--Delores, 38

_____**789.**

Some wine and cheese in bed is a
lovely way to get started.

--Sherea, 32

790._____

Look at me.

--Lora, 31

791._____

We've done it at his office lots of
times. I love that.

--Vicky, 39

792._____

I love a bed with posts I can hold
on to. That way we can do it as hard
as we want.

--Kattie, 34

_____

793.

I saw this movie where the couple had sex in the back of a limo--that's been my secret fantasy ever since.

--Angie, 32

794.

We don't just get undressed, we strip for each other.

--Stephanie, 31

795.

Afternoon rendezvous are what I live for.

--Marlene, 34

796._____

I love having my thighs massaged.

--Sally, 42

797._____

My husband can't help looking at other women, and I can't help being pissed when he does.

--Peg, 37

798._____

I can't believe it when he eats stuff like garlic and onions and then expects me to let him put his tongue in my mouth.

--Jane, 44

_____**799.**

I wish men wouldn't press so hard--
literally and figuratively.

--Maria, 29

_____**800.**

Once I was with a man who made
love to me standing up with me
wrapped around him. That was
fantastic.

--Kathryn, 26

_____**801.**

Sex on the beach is best.

--Sherry, 34

802._____

I'm looking for a feeling of
closeness, not an orgasm.

--Rene, 34

803._____

It turns me on to see other people
do it. I used to spy on my
roommate and her boyfriend in
college--now I rent porn videos.

--Linda, 28

804._____

I know I'm not a fashion model, but
I still like to hear I'm beautiful.

--Helen, 35

_____**805.**

Show me I'm important to you in other ways besides sex.

--*Victoria, 37*

_____**806.**

My boyfriend doesn't wear any underwear. That way he can whip it out whenever I want it.

--*Peggy, 25*

_____**807.**

A bubble bath before puts us in the perfect mood.

--*Cicily, 31*

_____

808.

Men who know how to dress are
instant eye-catchers.

--Caroline, 37

809.

Sex shouldn't be a power struggle.
I've never been interested in
hostile takeovers.

--Nancy, 44

810.

Sex in an elevator, especially a glass
one, is incredible.

--Kim, 23

811.

I can lay in bed all night and watch my husband make love to me in the mirror.

--Evelyn, 33

812.

Call me at work and let me know what to expect.

--Cara, 28

813.

Even after I'm in a relationship, I still like to be seduced.

--Marcia, 31

814._____

Kisses should be soft. All the
blood shouldn't be forced out of
my lips.

--*Barbra, 27*

815._____

I like food after sex.

--*Tracey, 32*

816._____

I need a man who adheres to *my*
arousal schedule.

--*Geena, 34*

_____817.

If I know I'm wanted, I feel sexy.

--Brenda, 36

_____818.

I know it's good when we're both sweating.

--Deena, 27

_____819.

We tickle each other until we can't stand it.

--Mollie, 26

820._____

Love my mind and my spirit first, and my body will follow.

--Leslie, 23

821._____

I like it when we're in the throes of passion and our fingers interlock. It's like we're totally one.

--Terry, 26

822._____

Mystery is the sexiest element in any person.

--Charlene, 41

823.

If I'm giving you oral sex, do not try to ram yourself down my throat.

--Judy, 29

824.

Sweat on a man is a big turn on for me.

--Lisa, 32

825.

When a guy's just gone down on me, I wish he wouldn't try to kiss me on the mouth.

--Shannon, 34

826.

I love to get him all hot and bothered when we're in public and he can't do anything about it. I really make him suffer for it.

--Veronica, 22

827.

He's not going to get oral sex every time we have sex. That's for when he's been an especially good boy.

--Glenda, 43

828.

I want someone I can be silly with.

--Sue, 31

829.

Turn off the television, please.

--Lila, 38

830.

I'll use a vibrator if I'm alone, but with a man I want it to be just the two of us.

--Becky, 31

831.

In sex, there's got to be an even amount of giving and taking.

--Selina, 35

832.

Having sex with me doesn't prove that you love me. I mean, it's not that much of a chore, is it?

--Judith, 31

833.

I've got to see his eyes when we do it.

--Janet, 26

834.

Every man can be a good lover if he makes love with his heart and not his penis.

--Cassi, 38

_____**835.**

Playful nibbling is very erotic.

--Alesa, 28

_____**836.**

I don't like to talk during sex. I'd rather get into the physical aspect of what's going on.

--Dorothy, 34

_____**837.**

I can tell how a man really feels about me by how different he acts after we've had sex.

--Tammy, 33

_____

838._____

The tackiest thing a guy can do is carry a condom inside his wallet.

--Brooke, 31

839._____

When I give in to sleeping with a man, I feel like I've lost some of the power I had in the relationship. I think that's part of what keeps me from achieving orgasm.

--Sharon, 34

840._____

He's got to be my friend first.

--Julia, 30

841.

There's a time and place for sex--
anytime and anywhere.

--Linda, 36

842.

Arrogance will get you nowhere.
Humility is the key.

--Joyce, 31

843.

Foot massages are my secret
pleasure.

--Blair, 34

844._____

Don't expect sex if you've been an ass all week.

--Nicole, 28

845._____

During sex, some guys get this look on their face like they can't believe they're finally doing it. That's awful.

--Andrea, 29

846._____

The best sex I ever had was at a party in the coat closet.

--Karen, 32

847.

Take my panties off nice and slow.

--Natalie, 30

848.

It's not what you can do for you, but what you can do for me.

--Felicia, 27

849.

Since my breasts are so big, I usually have to hold them to keep them from bouncing around. I like it when he holds them, though.

--Nikki, 29

850._____

It's great to fall asleep next to your lover and wake up next to your friend.

--Dinah, 42

851._____

I like doing it to music with a nice, steady beat. That way there's no confusion about who's rhythm to follow.

--Christel, 33

852._____

I'm a lot wilder with the lights off.

--Suzi, 34

853.

Men are looking for quantity sex, while women are looking for quality sex.

--Hope, 36

854.

Men are on a mission when it comes to sex. If they'd stop and enjoy, we'd both be better off.

--Jane, 32

855.

I need help from a man to feel sexy. Kind words mean a lot to me.

--Christina, 39

856.

Women have to give more of themselves during sex than a man does. That's why we're more selective about who we give it to.

--Bonita, 40

857.

I have to be laying on my side during intercourse to have an orgasm. It feels so much better.

--Terrelle, 36

858.

Most men are too rough in bed.

--Catherine, 26

859.

Men who call a woman "slut," "whore" or "bitch" when they're making love have seen too many porno movies.

--Ruth, 27

860.

Men's underwear that goes up their butt crack is just too much for me.

--Carla, 30

861.

Anything dipped in chocolate is going in my mouth.

--Suzanne, 32

862.

No teeth on my nipples.

--Dionne, 27

863.

Acting teachers will tell you how sometimes "less is more." I think the same rule applies to sex.

--LeAnna, 28

864.

I love it when he looks me in the eyes while he goes down on me.

--Candace, 31

865.

I do and say things in bed my mother would die over if she knew. That turns me on.

--Ronda, 26

866.

I make my husband pay for sex sometimes. For fifty bucks, he can do any little nasty thing he wants.

--Randi, 32

867.

I give pleasure more often than I get it. That needs to change.

--Joan, 38

868.

A sexy note or thoughtful card means a lot to me.

--Sallie, 35

869.

To me, great sex means great foreplay.

--Brigitte, 38

870.

Make lust to me.

--Ginny, 24

871.

I like to smother him between my legs.

--Evan, 35

872.

The best lovemaking is the daily contact--the hand-holding, hugs and kisses.

--Veronica, 31

873.

I love kisses on the small of my back.

--Annette, 42

874.

I'm totally submissive. I like him
to pin my wrists down and take me.

--Alice, 36

875.

Men take it so personally when I
tell them I won't swallow. If it
tastes so good, you swallow it.

--Diana, 27

876.

I feel safer when we're at *my*
apartment. Familiar surroundings
allow me to be myself.

--Kristy, 28

877.

I don't like for a man to be nicer than I am. I want a rough boy.

--Simone, 26

878.

The whole seduction process should be thought of as a game. If played right, we both win.

--Valerie, 34

879.

My husband loves oral sex. I'd like it too, if he'd offer.

--Meg, 32

880.

I get turned on when he paints my toenails.

--Millicent, 34

881.

I like it when he comes up behind me while I'm doing the dishes and starts ravishing me.

--Peggy, 35

882.

I'm very sensitive after I reach orgasm. I have to stop everything for a minute.

--Andrea, 26

_____**883.**

I know it sounds weird, but I like to have my belly button licked.

--Amanda, 29

_____**884.**

Call my name when you come.

--Samantha, 31

_____**885.**

He takes my panties off first, *then* he takes off my skirt.

--Jociline, 25

_____

886._____

Don't assume you know what I like
in bed. Ask me.

--Norene, 41

887._____

I don't care for wet, drooly kisses.

--Gretta, 26

888._____

I love it when he rubs his penis on
my thigh before he puts it in.

--Heather, 28

_____

889.

I'm glad I married a man who doesn't go to sleep immediately after sex. That's the worst.

--Lucille, 40

890.

I like making love on a waterbed. The motion of the water feels great.

--Mary, 28

891.

I love it when my boyfriend pulls down my bra and sucks my tits.

--Lynn, 30

892._____

Good dancers make good lovers.

--Falan, 29

893._____

Doggie-style, with some spanking
to go along with it.

--Carmen, 31

894._____

Respect me as a person.

--Kim, 33

_____

895.

I actually like reading those supposedly "true" letters in the men's magazines. They're wild.

--Ellie, 43

896.

I want to be man-handled a bit.

--Nancy, 34

897.

Some men try to hurt women during sex so they'll feel superior. There's no room in my bed for one of those.

--Cathy, 33

898._____

It's silly the way they're always
worried about the size of their
penis.

--Barbi, 36

899._____

Be careful not to pull out too far
and then accidentally put it
somewhere it's not supposed to go.

--Rosalee, 32

900._____

What's inside his head is what
counts. Not what's inside his pants.

--Tonia, 42

_____

_____**901.**

When I want to do it, I want to do it now.

--Torey, 22

_____**902.**

I like giving oral sex to guys with smaller penises. If it's too big, my jaw gets tired.

--Denise, 31

_____**903.**

We whisper to each other in bed.

--Christie, 28

904.

I like to be treated like a lady all the time--even during sex.

--Angel, 34

905.

It's awkward, but I've got to know your sexual history.

--Ann, 30

906.

I've had men and women, and the biggest difference is that women know to take it easy.

--Lynn, 34

907.

Sometimes it really is better to give than to receive.

--Joyce, 34

908.

I have to get to know someone before I jump into bed with him (or her).

--Rachel, 29

909.

I like my husband's attitude in bed-- he's there to have a good time just like me.

--Kay, 30

910.

A gentle touch to the face, the inner forearm, the calves, even the palms are all sexually stimulating. Not just according to me, but almost all of the women I've discussed it with.

--Cathy, 37

911.

The intimacy after is the thing.

--Marina, 43

912.

No TV.

--Teresa, 31

_____**913.**

Ask me what feels good.

--Lee, 34

_____**914.**

I like men with hair that I can play with.

--Sabrina, 23

_____**915.**

The missionary position is my favorite, and I think I've tried them all.

--Naomi, 27

_____

916._____

It's important to feel loved
constantly.

--Katherine, 30

917._____

I want it to last all night. An orgasm
for a man is like an itch he has to
scratch. I wish he'd let it itch for a
while longer, then I'd be happy to
scratch it for him.

--Kitty, 39

918._____

Respect me and my things.

--Dina, 33

_____

919.

When we made love in hopes of starting a family, the emotions ran even higher.

--Rebecca, 31

920.

The man has to bring me out of my shell. They always say it was worth the extra time it took.

--Joy, 29

921.

Men who have to get high in order to make love are not for me.

--Morgan, 26

922.

Let me make the first move.

--Tiffany, 34

923.

I love posing nude for him, like
I'm a centerfold girl. I get off on
seeing the pictures, too.

--Tina, 28

924.

More oral sex.

--Becky, 42

_____**925.**

The sounds a man makes when he reaches orgasm really get me hot.

--Lora, 20

_____**926.**

Bald men can be very sexy. Their heads are so smooth, it's sort of a turn on.

--Vicki, 34

_____**927.**

If a man treats me lovingly everyday, it's easier for me to love him that night.

--Susan, 26

928.

Let me know you're glad to be with me.

--Delores, 38

929.

The special bond you feel afterward is what makes it all worthwhile.

--Melanie, 21

930.

The kissing and hugging is what I'm after. I do the rest for him.

--Janie, 44

931.

Traveling and seeing new places always makes me want sex.

--Jessica, 32

932.

If a man can't remember my name, he's got no business in my bed.

--Paula, 35

933.

If he doesn't make the first move, nothing is going to happen.

--Kami, 31

934._____

Play around with my pubic hair.

--*Patsy, 28*

935._____

I appreciate subtleties.

--*Irene, 39*

936._____

More foreplay.

--*Clarissa, 22*

_____**937.**

I like it when he takes off my
jewelry.

--*June, 36*

_____**938.**

My husband and I play footsie
under the dinner table as a prelude
to making love.

--*Penny, 34*

_____**939.**

I can't resist him when he pulls my
panties off with his teeth.

--*Tracy, 27*

940._____

We have to be connecting mentally before we move on to the physical.

--Yvonne, 36

941._____

Not much aftershave. I don't want to smell him for the next two days.

--Marianne, 39

942._____

I love it when he puts his hands inside my panties and then slowly slides them off.

--Dale, 28

_____**943.**

All I'm really looking for is to be held.

--Kimberly, 29

_____**944.**

I love it when he licks my lips.

--Michelle, 24

_____**945.**

I don't buy into that "pleasure being pain" routine. If it hurts, it's not for me.

--Patricia, 32

_____

946._____

I'd rather have a finger inside me than a penis. It's easier to control and I won't get pregnant.

--Marion, 31

947._____

We take turns serving each other.

--Leila, 26

948._____

Sex is best when it's a celebration of love.

--Renee, 28

_____**949.**

It's important to laugh together.

--Karrie, 30

_____**950.**

I want a man with a sense of sexual adventure.

--Stephanie, 34

_____**951.**

The flirting should never end.

--Jeanne, 37

_____

952._____

I can't reveal too much about myself to a man until after I've slept with him.

--Amanda, 34

953._____

I've faked orgasm for two reasons-- to please one man and to get another one the hell off me.

--Karen, 37

954._____

Watching the sun come up while you're still out of breath from sex.

--Linda, 35

_____**955.**

Gentleness will get you everywhere.

--Beth, 27

_____**956.**

I love to run the bathtub faucet over my vagina.

--Patty, 23

_____**957.**

Edible panties are great.

--Connie, 24

_____

958._____

I want a man who can use both heads
at the same time.

--Glenda, 26

959._____

We masturbate in front of each
other.

--Deborah, 34

960._____

I like to wrap my legs around his
back and squeeze real tight.

--Carla, 23

_____

_____961.

Playful conversation in bed adds to
the fun of sex.

--Sherry, 32

_____962.

Sometimes, we'll pretend we're
meeting each other for the first
time.

--Amy, 34

_____963.

Most men engage in foreplay
because they think they have to. I
love a man who wants to.

--Darcy, 36

964._____

No sex is worth dying for. We've got
to use a condom with a spermicide.

--Genette, 27

965._____

I love it when we're kissing and he
guides my hand to his crotch.

--Kellie, 32

966._____

I (we) think sex is best when it's
shared with another couple. Love
from others strengthens our bond.

--Marsha, 39

_____

_____**967.**

I think familiarity makes for a
healthy love-life.

--Dawn, 30

_____**968.**

I tell all·my men to pull out before
they ejaculate. I like to see it
happen.

--Sheila, 28

_____**969.**

Shut up and do me.

--Leslie, 28

_____

970._____

Standard missionary, but with my
legs in between the man's.

--Raven, 26

971._____

Trust.

--Harley, 32

972._____

I get turned on sitting on a man's
lap.

--Ruthanne, 21

_____973.

I love to cradle a man's head in my lap and offer him a breast like he's a baby.

--Jodie, 33

_____974.

Sex is nothing more than playtime for adults.

--Carolyn, 36

_____975.

On a beach as the sun comes up.

--Cynthia, 24

976._____

Texture turns me on.

--Shanna, 27

977._____

Men who "play the field" can play
with themselves as far as I'm
concerned.

--Tess, 31

978._____

Big penis = lousy lover.

--Miki, 29

_____

979.

The old saying "variety is the spice of life" is true in the bedroom.

--Tammy, 45

980.

Unexpected surprises keep a relationship fresh.

--Eva Marie, 38

981.

Petting and old-fashioned "making out" are fun before we actually have sex.

--Brenda, 36

982.

So many men don't know how to listen--especially when it comes to sex. You tell them something and they nod their heads, then they go back to what they've always done.

--Kristine, 23

983.

Nothing's sexier than the ocean.

--Carrie, 34

984.

I make love the way I'd like to be made love to.

--Jacqueline, 40

_____**985.**

I leave obscene messages on his voice-mail.

--Clarice, 27

_____**986.**

Don't bring up former encounters.

--Terri, 29

_____**987.**

Touch my breasts and kiss my neck all at once.

--Fran, 26

_____

988.

It ruins it if he gets up and leaves right after.

--Leah, 30

989.

There's a look in a man's eyes when he's in love that can't be faked. I won't sleep with a man until I see that look.

--Constance, 34

990.

He's got to take care of his body.

--Elise, 24

_____**991.**

Up on the roof, under the sky is magnificent.

--Margret, 34

_____**992.**

When I come home from work, he washes my feet. It's very loving and gentle.

--Joan, 35

_____**993.**

I wish I didn't have to tiptoe around his insecurities.

--Louise, 38

_____

994._____

Sometimes I'm just in it for the sex.

--Anita, 28

995._____

In the rain on top of a picnic table.

--Mary Beth, 25

996._____

Little circles traced around my clitoris make the sparks fly.

--Sonya, 23

_____

997.

If he spent more time on foreplay, I could enjoy sex so much more.

--Sandra, 41

998.

To feel sexy, I have to feel feminine.   And that means I have to be treated with respect.

--Kathleen 38

999.

One night, my boyfriend couldn't get an erection, so he used the rest of his body to make love to me.

--Daphne, 32

1000._____

Women aren't as looks-oriented as men.

--Dorothy, 31

1001._____

"No" really does mean "no."

--Sybil, 25

_____

What's YOUR Sex Secret?

Do you have a specific technique, insight or observation that every man or woman should know? If so, take part in this ongoing survey!

1. Call the *1001 Sex Secrets Research Line* at:

 ## 1-800-398-1001

2. A recorded message will ask for your FIRST NAME ONLY and your age.

3. When instructed, answer one or both of the following questions:

> **"What is the one thing you wish your partner knew about sex?"**

> **"Think back to the best sex you have ever had. What made that experience better than any other?"**

That's it. Remember, you're **COMPLETELY ANONY-IOUS,** so don't be afraid to speak with total honesty. Thanks for your participation.